CONTENTS

Words in **bold** are in the glossary.

PEOPLE HAVE ALWAYS WANTED TO SHOW OFF THE FASTEST, COOLEST, NEWEST GADGETS. Inventors are willing to try new ideas and materials to make those gadgets. But even the best planners have some ideas that don't turn out well. Learn how even great inventions turned out to be disasters.

CHAPTER 1

EERIE VOICES

EDISON'S TALKING DOLL

Thomas Edison was a busy inventor from the United States. One of his most popular inventions was the phonograph. The phonograph was a device that used a needle to pick up sounds from a spinning cylinder. Then it played the sounds through a loudspeaker. The first sound his phonograph played was the nursery rhyme "Mary Had a Little Lamb".

Edison dreamed of inventing talking dolls as early as 1877. That same year, he invented the phonograph. In 1890, he made the dolls a reality. He put a mini phonograph inside each doll. Children turned a key on the back of the doll and the doll "spoke" nursery rhymes.

HOW THE PHONOGRAPH WORKED

1 A person speaks into the tube.

2 His or her voice causes a vibration. This pushes a needle back and forth in the pattern of the vibration, cutting grooves into a piece of metal foil.

3 The foil is wrapped around a cylinder, which is turned by a motor.

4 Another needle traces the grooves in the metal. Electrical impulses are created as the needle bounces along the grooves.

5 A horn converts the impulses into sound that can be heard.

How many?

Thomas Edison filed 1,093 US **patents** and held 2,332 total patents around the world. But Japanese inventor Shunpei Yamazaki has him beat. Yamazaki holds 16,836 active US patents and has been named the inventor of more than 28,000 different patents. Yamazaki works in the fields of computer science and physics.

Thomas Edison (1847–1931)

Edison's doll stood 56 centimetres (22 inches) tall and weighed 1.8 kilograms (4 pounds). The phonograph inside (right) was 18 cm (7 inches) tall.

At the time, a talking doll was astonishing. But the dolls were not very popular. They were expensive. Dolls with plain clothes cost $10. A doll with fancy clothes was $25, equal to about £400 in today's money.

The dolls said the same thing over and over. And they didn't sound nice. Even Edison described the voices as "exceedingly unpleasant".

The phonograph's cylinders were fragile and broke easily. This did not make them good toys for children.

Edison's concre-ations

Inventors are willing to try making new products and using new materials, even if they seem strange or unusual. Thomas Edison had a factory that made concrete. His concrete was used to build Yankee Stadium for the New York Yankees baseball team. He had so much concrete he invented other ways to use it. He designed a case for his popular phonograph that was made of concrete. He created a working piano that had a concrete cabinet. He even had plans to build whole houses from concrete. But an invention isn't a success unless people like it and use it.

Edison made 10,000 dolls. But he sold fewer than 500. People didn't like the dolls and returned them. Records show that around 7,500 dolls were never moved from storage.

Lessons learned

The technology wasn't right for talking toys during Edison's lifetime. Other talking toys came and went. After the invention of electronic microchips, though, talking toys became a hit.

CHAPTER 2
PLAYBACK PROBLEMS
THE LASERDISC

Sometimes even really great inventions are considered failures. They may get the job done, but if another similar invention does the job a little bit better, they fail. The LaserDisc is an example of this type of invention.

David Paul Gregg invented the technology for LaserDiscs in 1958. He received a patent for it in 1961. A LaserDisc is a plastic disc about 31 centimetres (12 inches) wide. Lasers burn a sequence of holes into the disc to record sounds and images.

The LaserDisc solved some of the problems with film **projectors**. Film projectors were difficult to use. Rolls of film were large and heavy. Sometimes filmstrips tore or broke. The LaserDisc made it easier for people to watch films at home. The invention also made it easier for schools to show films.

To watch films at home or at school, people needed a special LaserDisc player. A laser in the player read the code and transformed the information into sounds and images.

The Philips company released LaserDiscs to the public in 1978. They worked really well. The quality of the images and sounds was good.

Jaws was the first film recorded onto a LaserDisc.

But there were a few problems. The LaserDiscs were large. Each disc weighed about 225 grams (8 ounces). They were also fragile. Their short running time was another problem. Only an hour of video could be played on each side. And LaserDisc players were very expensive.

A new technology had arrived a year before LaserDiscs became available. The video cassette was a rectangular plastic case with a videotape inside.

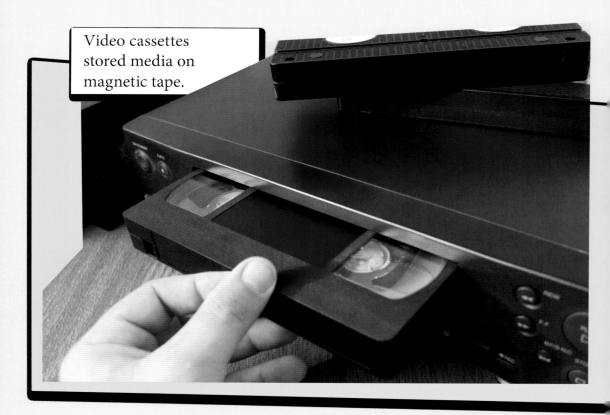

Video cassettes stored media on magnetic tape.

Video cassettes could hold several hours of video. The picture was not as high quality as one from a LaserDisc. But they were cheaper. LaserDiscs cost five times more to make.

And video cassettes could do something LaserDiscs couldn't do – they were recordable. People could record programmes from their televisions onto the video cassettes. People could even watch one series on one channel and record onto a video cassette from a different channel.

Lessons learned

LaserDiscs did what they were supposed to do. But video cassettes did the job just a little bit better. So even though LaserDiscs worked, they were still a failed invention. But the technology used to create LaserDiscs was important. It helped companies create other new technologies such as CDs, DVDs, **Blu-ray** and more.

CHAPTER 3
MOVIES IN THE DARK
POLAVISION

Inventors often know what people want, but don't have the technology to create a product that people love.

People in the mid-to-late 1900s loved their Polaroid cameras. With other cameras, people had to take their film to a developer and wait several days for their photographs. But Polaroid cameras developed their photographs instantly.

People also loved taking home movies. In the 1970s, people recorded films and home movies with sound on Super 8 film. But like ordinary camera film, Super 8 film still had to be developed.

What if people could make films at home that could be developed instantly? In 1977, Polaroid introduced Polavision.

The product was easy to use. The film was stored in a **cartridge**. The cartridge was easy to load into the handheld camera. The film was in colour. It looked like a great product.

FACT: The first Polaroid camera was sold in 1948 for $89.95. By 1956, more than 1 million had been sold. The first colour Polaroid film was created in 1963.

Inventor Edwin Land shows off the Polavision in 1977.

The Polavision Viewer had a 31-cm (12-inch) screen. The colours in the picture were so dense that the home movies could not be projected onto a larger screen.

But there were big problems. The film could only record for two and a half minutes, and there was no sound. If people filmed in low light, the images weren't clear. And a special Polavision player was needed to see their short, silent and possibly dark home movies.

Polaroid only sold Polavision cameras and projectors for two years. The company lost a lot of money on this gadget disaster.

FACT: The cartridge was a self-contained film processing centre. A pod of developing liquid was inside. Placing the cartridge in the viewer started the processing. It took about a minute to complete.

The first home videos

The first video recording technology was invented in the 1920s. The first videotape recorder (VTR) was sold in 1956. It cost $50,000. The first video cassette recorder (VCR) for home use was sold in 1971.

By the 1980s, both Polavision and Super 8 films had faded from the market. Video cassettes and handheld video cameras made it easy to take home movies and watch them at home.

Lessons learned

The idea of instant home movies people could watch straight away was a good one. But the technology just wasn't there to make a product that worked well. Longer videos, easier ways to watch them, better picture quality and sound would have made a big difference.

CHAPTER 4

DISPOSABLE OUTFITS
PAPER CLOTHING

Some inventors take two things that have been around for a long time and blend them together to create a new and exciting idea. This idea can transform people's lives, or it can be a total flop. Some ideas are in the middle.

People have worn clothing for thousands of years. And people have used paper for centuries. So why not use paper clothing?

This was a real invention that became a hit in the 1960s. By 1967, people could buy paper clothing in top department stores. Clothing companies made all kinds of paper clothes. Men had paper vests. Women wore paper bridal gowns. Children even had paper clothes. There were paper swimming costumes, although they only lasted one or two wears.

Paper clothes were inexpensive and very interesting. Many had eye-catching, artistic designs. Some even had patterns that buyers could colour in themselves. Fashion designers turned it into high-end **couture**.

Party time

Paper clothing was first created for hospital use. It was hygienic and could be thrown away after being used. Later, paper companies made paper dresses to match the party supplies they were selling, such as paper cups, tablecloths and napkins. The pattern of the dresses matched the pattern on the paper tableware. Sometimes the dresses would come with vouchers for other paper products.

Fashion models in Paris showed off a line of paper outfits in 1967.

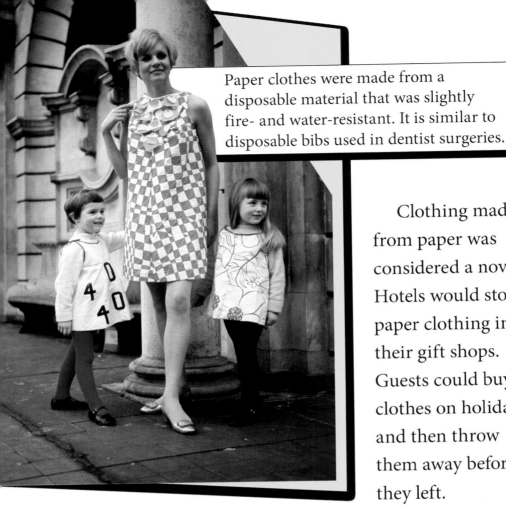

Paper clothes were made from a disposable material that was slightly fire- and water-resistant. It is similar to disposable bibs used in dentist surgeries.

Clothing made from paper was considered a novelty. Hotels would stock paper clothing in their gift shops. Guests could buy clothes on holiday and then throw them away before they left.

Paper clothes didn't last as long as real clothing or as a fashion trend. They weren't very comfortable. They didn't fit very well. Sometimes the colours wore off. They were also **flammable**. Although outfits could be refreshed by a quick iron, the heat from the iron often removed any protection against water or fire originally added to the material. People worried about wearing clothing that could easily catch fire.

People wore them once or twice, then threw the clothes away. The disposable nature made people believe they weren't worth the money. Paper clothing disappeared from clothes shops by 1968.

Lessons learned

Some inventions are only popular for a short time. These ideas are trends. They show inventors that people are willing to experiment and try new things. But if an idea isn't practical, it won't last.

Invented before its time

Sometimes an inventor has a great idea but it takes a while to catch on. In 1902, Mary Anderson was on a streetcar in New York City. She noticed that the driver had to keep getting out to wipe snow off the streetcar's window. She wondered if there was a way for snow to be removed without stopping the car. So she developed hand-operated windscreen wipers. When she tried to sell her invention to car companies, they were not interested. But after 1920, more and more people owned cars, and the car companies finally recognized the value of windscreen wipers.

CHAPTER 5
READING IT WRONG
READAMATIC ROBOT

Many inventions are meant to solve problems that people face. But sometimes inventions cause more problems than they solve. The Readamatic Robot was the perfect example of an unhelpful invention.

The Readamatic Robot was invented in 1963. It was a device made of a small box and metal arm with a second metal bar at one end. The metal arm stretched over the page in a book. The metal bar sat on a page under the words. As a person read, the Readamatic Robot arm moved down the page.

One goal of the Readamatic Robot was to help people read faster. The second goal was to help struggling readers slow down and understand more of what they read.

The Readamatic Robot could be adjusted to fit different books with different numbers of words per page. By turning a knob on the box, readers could change the speed of the metal bar. They could speed it up or slow it down.

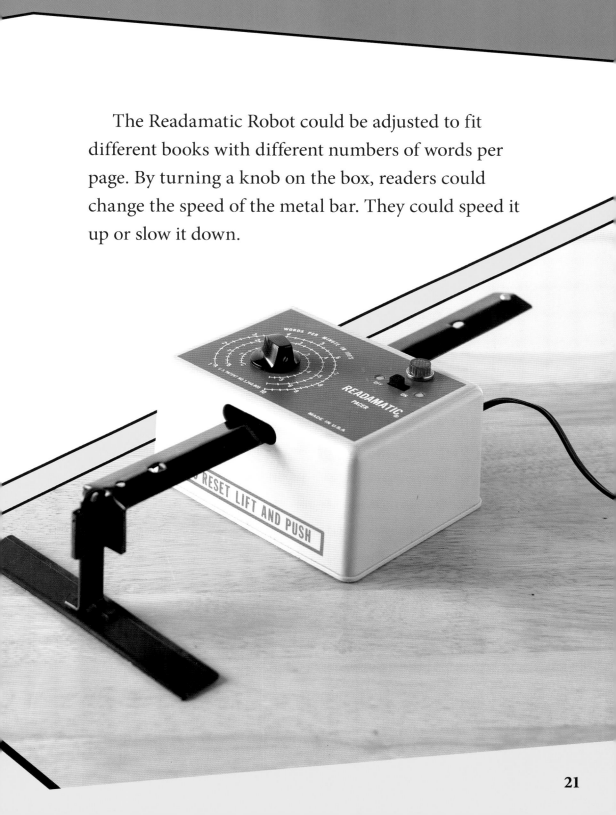

Although the idea of a robot to help people read was a good one, the Readamatic Robot was a bad gadget.

The Readamatic Robot could be adjusted from a reading pace of 100 words a minute to 1,000.

The sound of the metal bar scratching on the page was distracting. The whirring of the motor was distracting too. The long metal arm blocked part of the page. In the end, the same result could be created by readers holding a ruler under the lines as they read.

Lessons learned

Sometimes things designed to help actually create more of a problem. Instead of helping people to read, the Readamatic Robot made it harder for them to concentrate.

Helpful robots

Some robots are very helpful. The first robot vacuum cleaner came out in 1996. Now they are popular. They use a variety of **sensors** to move around homes and clean up dirt. Some have special brushes or use **ultraviolet** (UV) technology to kill germs. Some are specially designed to clean carpets or mop hard floors.

CHAPTER 6

WHEN YOUR PHONE BLOWS UP

SAMSUNG GALAXY NOTE 7 BATTERIES

Most of the time, a gadget disaster just means a new idea doesn't work. But some gadget disasters can cause serious damage and even put people in danger.

In August 2016, Samsung launched a new model of a smartphone called the Note 7. The phone had received great advance reviews. Pre-orders were at a record high. Samsung forecasted it would ship 15 million phones around the world before the end of the year.

Soon after people started using the new phones, though, they noticed there was a huge problem. Some of the phones unexpectedly exploded and burst into flames. People were injured by the fires. One fire destroyed a person's vehicle. Another fire caused the evacuation of an aeroplane. Eventually, the phone was banned on all flights.

The company acted quickly. Fourteen days after its launch, sales were suspended. A **recall** was sent out. Replacement phones were sent out by the end of September. But then the replacement phones also started catching fire!

Mobile phone batteries are designed to store as much energy as they can. If that energy is suddenly released, phones can melt and fires can start.

Investigators learned that the batteries in the phones caused the explosions and fires. Samsung purchased the batteries from two different **manufacturers**. The two different types of batteries had two different problems.

In one battery, the positive and negative **electrodes** touched and caused a **short circuit**. The other battery had a sharp edge inside. That edge pierced the battery's insulation and caused a short circuit. The short circuits were what caused the fires.

Samsung ended up sending out an update that would **brick** all Note 7s. They asked Note 7 customers to return their phones. In the end, the loss of pre-sales, profits and future sales hurt the company. The Note 7 cost Samsung £13 billion.

Lessons learned

Samsung acted quickly to contact customers and recall the dangerous batteries. But if they hadn't acted so quickly to release the phone in the first place, engineers would have had more time to discover potential problems. The promise of a smaller phone with a larger battery wasn't something that could be delivered quickly.

Samsung shared information with other manufacturers to help prevent these sorts of problems in future technology. Manufacturers also agreed to do even more testing on technology to ensure its safety before selling to consumers.

CHAPTER 7

BOOST ME UP
BELL ROCKET BELT

In the 1950s, Wendell Moore had an idea. He decided the world needed a rocket booster pack to help people leap long distances. As an employee at Bell Aerosystems, a huge **aviation** company, he had the skills and resources to make that possible.

The first Bell Rocket Belt looked like a large rucksack with handles. It had a fuel tank and two nozzles. The fuel tank held 19 litres (5 gallons) of concentrated hydrogen peroxide. When the pilot pressed the controls, fuel was forced out of the tanks. The fuel reacted with silver plates, which turned it into highly pressurized steam. The steam exited through the nozzles and lifted the pilot into the air.

In early test flights, the pilot and rocket booster pack often wobbled and went off balance. The pilot and rocket belt were attached to a safety tether so they would not fly too high.

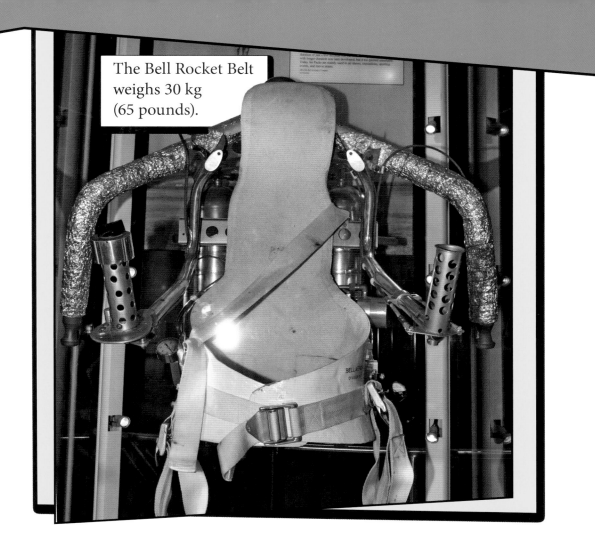

The Bell Rocket Belt weighs 30 kg (65 pounds).

Moore was one of the test pilots. During one demonstration, his pack tilted and broke the tether. Moore fell from the air. He broke his kneecap. After that, Moore didn't make any more test flights. But he didn't stop working on the Rocket Belt.

The new test pilot, Harold Graham, practised over and over. He could launch 1.2 metres (4 feet) in the air and zoom about 31 metres (100 feet) forwards before landing. The first flight lasted 13 seconds. Eventually, he learned how to fly in a circle, soar over cars and slip between trees. But the belt itself didn't improve much. Its flight time was a maximum of 21 seconds.

The US Army wanted to see the belt in 1961. But officials weren't impressed. The flight time was too short. Inventors worked on a new version that used superheated water vapour for fuel.

Successful water pistols

Another inventor who didn't give up after one try was Lonnie Johnson. In 1986, Lonnie received a patent for a device he called the "Power Drencher". It combined a water bottle with a water pistol. It used air pressure to shoot water further than an ordinary water pistol. Eventually, it was renamed the Super Soaker and has been a huge success.

That didn't help. The fuel was so hot that pilots had to wear insulating clothes to protect themselves from burns. In addition, the height the belt flew at was too low for a parachute to work. If the engine failed in the sky, the pilot would probably be injured.

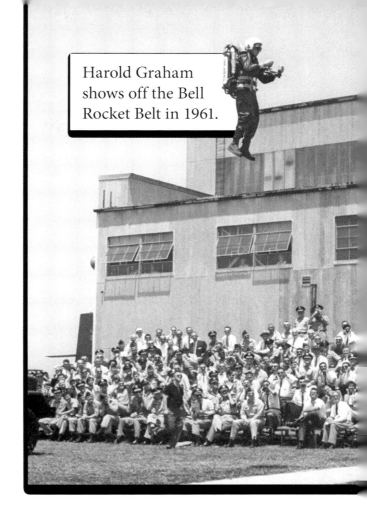

Harold Graham shows off the Bell Rocket Belt in 1961.

Lessons learned

Even though the Bell Rocket Belt didn't take off as Moore had hoped, it is still being used, mostly for entertainment. It has been used during events at Disneyland, in the opening ceremonies for the 1984 and 1996 Summer Olympics, and in a James Bond film.

CHAPTER 8
FLAILING FINGERS RING

Wearable technology sounds really exciting. Some people wear headphones on their ears or smart watches on their wrists. The company Logbar promised people they could have the power of technology at their fingertips – literally! Logbar's product, a large silver ring, would connect with a smartphone. The wearer could get alerts, send texts, change the phone's volume, turn on lights, or even pay bills with gestures.

In 2014, the still-small company raised money through **crowdfunding**. Its goal was $250,000. More than 5,000 people contributed. The campaign raised $880,000 in 36 days.

Ring wearers could trace letters in the air with their fingers. The letters would be translated into texts.

Ring premiered at Japan's first wearable technology expo in 2014.

Wash your hands!

Sometimes the simplest solution isn't a new invention. Inventor Philipp Zumtobel didn't like the smudges on his phone screen, so he invented Phone Fingers. But these little rubber finger covers were too hard to put on and take off. The simplest solution to dirty phone screens was to only use the phone with clean hands.

When people got their Ring, they were disappointed. Many people felt it was too thick to wear comfortably on a finger. It also only came in three sizes, which limited who could use it. When users tried gesturing, most of the time nothing happened.

Smart eyewear

Many inventors and companies are working on new types of wearable tech. Google introduced Google Glass. Google Glass is wearable smart technology that looks like glasses.

Doctors have used Google Glass and other smart technology to record and store the operations they perform. Others have used them to livestream procedures to medical schools around the world.

People had concerns. Some worried the device would invade their privacy if users recorded conversations without permission. Businesses were worried Google Glass might help users break the law, such as by recording films in cinemas. But doctors, journalists and people with autism and vision problems have benefited from Google Glass.

In order to activate Ring, users pressed a small button on the side of the device. A small LED light flashed to show that Ring was ready. But the light didn't always work. Other people reported that it refused to pair with their other smart technology.

People learned that the app always had to be open on their smartphones for an action to work. In order to control household appliances, people had to buy another device called the Ring Hub.

Instead of turning on a phone, connecting Ring and trying a gesture that might not do anything, it was easier for people to just use their smartphones by themselves.

Lessons learned

The idea for Ring was a good one. But the execution was a fail. It was too bulky and too inconvenient to use. The technology didn't work all the time, and it wasn't as futuristic as promised. But that didn't stop other inventors. Today there are smart rings that track your activity levels, heart rate and body temperature. Others allow you to pay for things, lock your car and get access to your online accounts.

CHAPTER 9
A REAL STINKER!
SMELL-O-VISION

The first films were a treat for the eyes, and later the ears. Why not the nose too?

In the 1920s and 1930s, some cinema owners experimented with blowing smells into cinemas while people watched films. In big cinemas, not everyone smelled the odours. Sometimes the scents mixed and did not smell nice, or lingered for a long time.

Inventor Hans Laube had a plan. His idea was to send scents to each individual seat in the cinema. He shared his first idea for "Scentovision" at the 1939 New York World's Fair. No one was interested.

Laube didn't get discouraged. In 1954, he filed for a patent for Smell-O-Vision. Smell-O-Vision was controlled by the "smell brain". The smell brain was a circular belt with little perfume capsules. As the film played, the smell brain rotated under the seats. At certain points during the film, a needle pierced the capsules. Fans blew the scents up to the viewer.

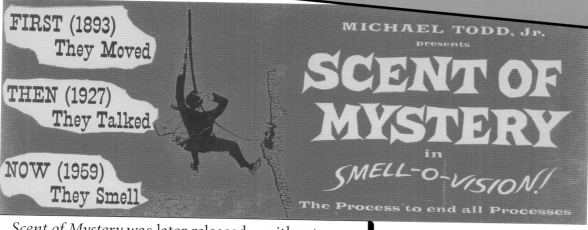

FIRST (1893)
They Moved

THEN (1927)
They Talked

NOW (1959)
They Smell

MICHAEL TODD, Jr.
presents

SCENT OF
MYSTERY
in
SMELL-O-VISION!

The Process to end all Processes

Scent of Mystery was later released – without smells – under the name *Holiday in Spain*.

In the late 1960s, Laube met film producer Mike Todd Jr. Todd helped make the first film to use Smell-O-Vision, *Scent of Mystery*. There was a peach smell for the scene in the peach orchard. There was a grape aroma for the scene when a wine barrel fell off a cart. When one character was on screen, viewers could smell tobacco.

Smelly competition

At the same time Smell-O-Vision launched, another company offered film smells. AromaRama blew scents through the cinema's air conditioning system. It included 72 smells to pair with the film *Behind the Great Wall*. People called this competition between the two films the battle of the "smellies".

37

Smell-O-Vision worked, but it wasn't perfect. The machine hissed as it released smells. People complained the scents didn't reach them. There was loud sniffing as viewers tried to catch the scent, which bothered their neighbours.

TIMELINE OF ON-SCREEN SUCCESSES

French inventor Louis Le Price releases a 2.11-second film called *Roundhay Garden Scene*. It is the world's earliest surviving film.

1888

The Story of the Kelly Gang is the first full-length feature film.

1906

35mm film is invented. This allows cinemas to send films around the world.

1909

The Jazz Singer becomes the first full-length film with sound.

1927

1933

The first drive-in cinema opens.

1953

The House of Wax is released as the first colour 3-D film. It is also one of the first horror films to be shot in colour.

1967

Film-makers experiment with projecting high-resolution images onto multiple huge screens. The idea turned into what we know as Imax today. The first Imax cinema was built in 1971.

Even when technical problems with the smell brain were fixed, too many people had complaints. To add insult to injury, the film didn't get good reviews.

Lessons learned

Smell-O-Vision was set up in only three cinemas, and it was such a failure that no other cinemas wanted to try. The creators tried to improve the film's problems, but by then word had spread. Audiences couldn't be bothered to see Scent of Mystery.

Inventors have not given up on mixing films and smells, though. Some film-makers produced scratch-and-sniff cards that people scratched during the film. Others created devices that attach to computers and release smells when people visit certain websites. This idea may be waiting for the right inventor.

CHAPTER 10
OUT OF THE WAY!

SEGWAY

Some gadgets work really well. They do just what the inventor hoped. But if there's not a market for them, they won't sell.

The Segway is an electric vehicle. It has two wheels, a platform and a handlebar. A person rides a Segway by standing on the platform and holding on to the handles. With the smallest of motions, the Segway moves forwards or backwards.

Inventor Dean Kamen launched the Segway in 2001. At first, people were excited about this new way to get around. The Segway worked just as the developers said it would.

It was hoped that the Segway would become a new mode of transport. Adverts claimed it would become a part of everyday life, just like mobile phones and the internet.

SEGWAY PARTS

handlebar
riders hold the handlebar
when the Segway is in motion

steerable frame
controls the Segway; the rider
leans on the frame to turn

height adjustment knob
adjusts the handlebar height

mats
protect the sensors
underneath; provide a
comfortable standing
surface for the rider

indicator lights
indicate whether the Segway
is ready to ride; show
battery power

mud guards
keep mud, rocks
and sand from
flying up in the air

power base and batteries
Segways have two batteries; they need
to be charged after 12 hours of use

wheels
how the Segway
moves

There were some drawbacks to the wonder machine. It came with at least a £4,800 price tag, which was more than some secondhand cars!

Another issue was that the Segway was a unique-looking vehicle. Riders thought they might look silly riding one. Helmets and safety pads were recommended accessories. If it rained or snowed, there was no way to escape getting wet. You could easily hop off a scooter or skateboard and go inside in bad weather. But it's harder to move a 45-kilogram (100-pound) Segway.

FACT: Segway inventor Dean Kamen had other successes. The AutoSyringe helped people with diabetes get insulin. In 2005, he was inducted into the National Inventors Hall of Fame.

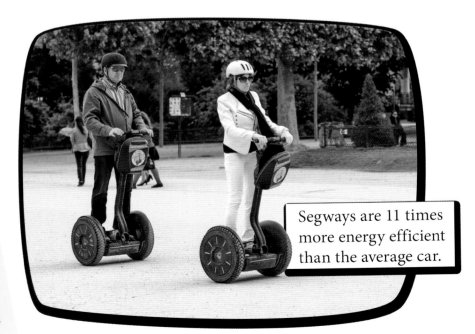

Segways are 11 times more energy efficient than the average car.

People had other questions too. Where would you park it? Where would you charge the battery? Where could you ride one? Its top speed was 20 kilometres (12.5 miles) per hour – too slow for the road, but too fast for the pavement. Some cities ended up banning Segways on both.

In the end, the biggest problem was that people didn't really need a Segway. It was a novelty, but not something they wanted to use on a regular basis.

Lessons learned

Even though the Segway worked well, it did not change the way people live or work on a daily basis. And owning one could be a challenge. Some places considered them to be motor vehicles and required them to be registered and insured. Some places required the rider to be licensed. Some didn't allow riders to carry any packages or baggage while riding. Police officers didn't know whether they should tell riders to get on or off the pavement. It is a successful invention but a failed innovation.

INVENTIONS BY KIDS

Not all inventors are adults. Kids invent things that have made life easier, more fun and less challenging.

Kylie Simonds was 8 years old when she was diagnosed with cancer. While she received chemotherapy, she had to push a heavy IV pole around. The wires were easy to trip over. Kylie invented a portable IV backpack in 2014. She is still working on making it available to the public.

Suman Mulumudi was at secondary school when he designed an iPhone case for people with medical conditions. It turns smartphones into stethoscopes using the phone's microphone. Patients can check their heart health and send information to their doctors.

In 2012, **Catherine Wong**, 17, came up with a way to help doctors see patients' heartbeats on a smartphone screen. Usually, a person's heartbeat is monitored with an electrocardiogram (EKG) machine. But they are usually only found at a doctor's surgery or a hospital. Catherine's invention would make it possible for anyone to gather that data anywhere, at any time. This is especially helpful in parts of the world where there are no hospitals.

In 1930, 16-year-old **George Nissen** first saw trapeze artists fall safely into a net. The net stretched and bounced the artists high into the air. Nissen wondered if he could make something that would let a person bounce longer. He built a prototype trampoline in 1937. Today trampolines are available to everyone.

Frank Epperson was 11 when he forgot his soft drink outside in the cold. He had left a stirring stick in the glass. When he discovered it in the morning, he saw it was frozen solid but fun to lick. Epperson patented the ice lolly in 1924.

In 1850, 12-year-old **Margaret E. Knight** was working at a cotton mill when she saw a young boy killed by machinery. She invented a safety mechanism that was soon installed in mills. Her invention saved lives.

In 1999, **Cassidy Goldstein** realized she could keep using worn-down crayons by holding them in small tubes that are used to keep flower stems fresh. Her invention helped reduce crayon waste. In 2006, she won the Youth Inventor of the Year award.

GLOSSARY

aviation industry that builds aeroplanes

Blu-ray digital storage format that uses compact discs

brick make a smartphone or other electronic device completely, and usually permanently, unusable

cartridge container holding a spool of photographic film

couture fashionable clothes that are made to measure to a person's specific size and style requirements

crowdfunding funding a project or business by raising small amounts of money from many people, usually over the internet

electrode point where an electric current can flow into or out of an object

flammable likely to catch fire

manufacturer person or company that makes products

patent legal document giving someone sole rights to make or sell a product

projector device used to project an image onto a large surface such as a screen or wall

recall official order to return a faulty product

sensor device that detects change in something such as heat, light, sound or motion

short circuit connection of lower resistance that is accidentally made between points on a circuit where the resistance is usually much greater; short circuits can occur when electrical wires or connections are damaged

ultraviolet rays of light that cannot be seen by the human eye

FIND OUT MORE

BOOKS

100 Inventions That Made History, DK (DK Children, 2014)

Gadgets and Games (Design and Engineering), Chris Oxlade (Raintree, 2014)

Great British Inventions (Best of British!), Claire Throp (Raintree, 2018)

Great Electronic Gadget Designs 1900 – Today (Iconic Designs), Ian Graham (Raintree, 2015)

WEBSITES

www.bbc.co.uk/bitesize/articles/zhn6wty
Find out more about some gadgets from the 1980s.

www.dkfindout.com/uk/science/famous-scientists
Learn more about some of the world's most famous scientists and inventors.

INDEX